D0552842

Hey Bert

Roberto Pastore studied in Carlisle, Cumbria, where he participated in the renowned Speakeasy spoken word scene. A chapbook of his poetry, *The Dumb Supper*, was released by Freerange Poetry in 2008. Roberto lives in Cardiff, where he works as a school crossing guard.

Instagram: @bertpastore

Hey Bert

Roberto Pastore

PARTHIAN

Parthian, Cardigan SA43 1ED www.parthianbooks.com
First published in 2019
© Roberto Pastore 2019
ISBN 978-1-912109-34-0
Editor: Susie Wild
Cover Image by Molly Sinclair-Thomson
Cover design by Emily Courdelle
Author photo by Jon Pountney
Typeset by Elaine Sharples
Printed and bound by 4edge Limited, UK
Published with the financial support of the Books Council of Wales
British Library Cataloguing in Publication Data
A cataloguing record for this book is available from the British Library.

To Siân,
hey siân

In loving memory of Nick Pemberton,
thanks for the typewriter, and everything

'Move the body repeatedly and you will start knowing yourself'

– Michelle Stuart

CONTENTS

THROAT

3 SALUTATION
4 THIS IS HOW THE DAY STARTS
6 A CAREFULLY PLACED HAND
9 GRASMERE WAY
10 THE INCOMING
12 DARK FLOW
15 A PREFIX
17 THE CONVULSION
22 PAST EXTENDS
25 LIONHEART
26 SHOW HOMES
27 AND NO GENERATION WON
30 THE PRIMARY BRIDE
31 YOUTH

BELLY

35 THE CONTENTS OF A HUMAN BODY
39 ONE FISH
41 PINK LIGHT
43 KNOCKING FROM THE HERE ALONE
46 NEW BOY
51 PARADISE ISLAND
54 VIVIAN SLEEPING
56 JUDAS STEER
58 HOW TO TAKE A BATH
59 THE TRICK WITH FLIES
60 A NEXT TIME

HEART

63 JUST SO YOU KNOW

64 CHRISTMASTIME IN BUTE PARK

65 YOU WERE THE ONLY ONE I WOULD'VE STAYED BEHIND
    FOR WHEN I KNEW IT WAS TIME TO GO

67 THERE IS A WORLD BELOW

68 THEN AGAIN

69 THIS DECISIVE ARC

71 HEART POEM

72 INFUSE WITH CHAMOMILE, LAVENDER & CATNIP

73 YOU GET USED TO IT

74 AN ENDLESS SUPPLY

75 FINALLY

76 THIS ONE THING

78 NOTES

79 ACKNOWLEDGEMENTS

THROAT

SALUTATION

It will start on an ordinary day.
You'll wake at dawn, the birds will be singing,
it won't even register.
You might notice a sensation
in the tips of your fingers, you might hear
a faint buzzing. It might be coming from somewhere far
away, or very near.
In the bath as you place your hands
underwater you notice
a golden glow
beneath your fingernails. As you hold them up out
of the water it subsides but doesn't go away completely.
As you step outside, into the quiet street,
the feeling will shift again. It might manifest as a
pain in your abdomen or genitals, like hundreds of
tiny spots popping. Steady yourself, it will pass, walk
into the light.
Keep walking, the sun is rising. Your fingertips are
dazzling, you can feel
gold pulsing and swimming up your arm
and down through your spine. Your skin tingles.
The birds go mute. Only
a steady hum now, though not from any power lines or
train tracks or radios. You are its source.
You will disregard what you were told as
a child, you will look directly into the sun.
You will know
that this is what is intended of you. As it rises now,
over the rooftops, over the trees, open your mouth.
Open wide, don't gag. Don't gag. You were waiting for
this day. Or something like it.

THIS IS HOW THE DAY STARTS

first you have to believe in the morning

that it exists and you exist

and that each bears its own homecoming
indigenous to the other

soon you will pass into the unlit

as you cup some of yesterday's shame in your open palms
remember everyone hates a mime

everyone hates a mime

but there you are
and you brought the day with you on your back

with its packed light, transmitting everything

everything
is transmitting

transmitting
everything

everything is transmitting everything

we have set up camp

we have waited so long

we have stared at rivers moonlit

we have baited the fish to catch the ocean

if our lives were out of focus

was it because we stood too far back from them?

did we forget ourselves along the way?

everything radiates from the shapes we pass through

o this is how the day starts

wasn't it always a long shot?

no, we were supposed to meet here in this moment, clean
and in flame

in this place

no longer on our knees

conceding no longer to life

A CAREFULLY PLACED HAND

let's practice attachment

a carefully placed hand

a carefully placed hand

a hand and a surface coalesce
self meet self

a congregation

look at your own hands now please palm up

the flexion creases the lunula

getting used to your hands

self meet self

now let's practice attachment

it's easy

touch me

make me unspecific

touch me

make me unspecific

do the coathanger let your wrists go limp

touch me make me unspecific

the more you dance the less specific

in all aspects of being we are wanting in all aspects of wanting we
will be fulfilled and now I'm going to dance for you

wanting to be touched wanting to be smoothed

the heel of the hand is what you stand on

a hand and a surface self meet self

getting used to your hands

smile when your body is smiling

we never smile when our bodies are smiling

all it takes to be complete

to be complete

to feel complete

all it takes

a finger in the bellybutton

fly the umbilical kite

fly the umbilical kite

when carefully placed

your hands are relief-givers are non-verbal relief-givers

touch me make me unspecific

touch me
make me unspecific

the more we dance the less specific

let's start our day by rubbing our hands together to
make them warm

self meet self

I am reaching up to the top cupboard for the oats

I shake the rice milk

now I am making porridge

practising attachment

practising attachment to the morning

my fingers are a congregation don't let my hands become derelict

going to send my untouched body out walking going to
send my human body out walking

going to dance for you

(touch me)

going to smile when my body is smiling

(make me unspecific)

going to sanctify you with a carefully placed hand

GRASMERE WAY

You passed me on Grasmere Way, it was
the summer of Jerry Garcia's heart attack, Tracey Emin's
tent, the drought.
The heat
made me feel guilty in a way that I couldn't
comprehend. My mother up all night, newly divorced,
looking at the sky.

You were the amateur morningstar,
lovesick and out for a drive, music blaring
from your stereo, tooting your horn at me, dipshit,
just sixteen years old.

I was halfway up Grasmere Way when the
sky darkened, the wind picked up.

Laughing with relief, I looked up as
the first drop landed on my shirt sleeve,
the rainsmell on the grey slanting road
immediately reminded me of all the rainfalls of my life.

I stood there
absolved
as your car ate the cracked light.

THE INCOMING

Two floors up, the fog, *only the fog*
could penetrate
my remoteness, your remoteness, the remoteness of
us, that room, at that time. No one, not a single body, could
get through to you.

They tried though, they all tried; the drunks,
the dogs, the incoming.

And me, I tried too. Not too hard I admit, I never
did anything with much oomph, you know this
about me, I am prone to headaches.
But I was so graceful and bloom-limbed then, angel
nothing steadied me like your boxer's shoulders your
deathbed stare.

On floorboards sun-whitened and stacked
with books, under Afghan crochet, by
fountain grass and
dirty plates, we'd drowse, our diet then
was crackers and posh peanut butter.

And the fog, that Scotch Street fog,
moved up against your one dark window,
while down below
the drunks, the dogs, the incoming.
Darkening against the unscheduled light, you'd rub
away sleep and stretch,

unlatch the root and bark between your legs,
draw the curtains.

The city would fuse with the room.

If it was us against them, then, if it was us
against those office-bound, sad-hearted,
cowed, morning-drenched
masses.

If it had been us only against them, then maybe

angel, our small love
might have faintly triumphed.

DARK FLOW

when I first saw you I said hello make me visible
hello I said make me visible
from the zone of avoidance make me visible
under the white anguish of clouds make me visible
purge my longing make me visible
with cascara bark and rhubarb root purge me
o make me visible
move me with your dark flow
I bought limes to make lime water but the limes went sour
my cat died in my arms I saw the dark flow out
my beautiful baby who will hold your belly now
unplugging my head for the light to escape
unplugging my chest so I can receive your dark flow
let me receive your dark flow
drinking lime water in your bed falling asleep to the sound of the
stars pulling our wormy lives in their tightgrip
I'm talking to the space in front of me now make me visible
now I'm by the water fountain make me visible
where the water stands up make me visible
where the water rises up into the water bearer's jug what is that,
is it dark flow?
will the dark flow rise up into the emptiness and make us visible?
something birdlike in the spirit-dividing air
something feral but with the eyes of a guidance counsellor
now I'm moving faster the particles you left behind are
bouncing off of me
now I'm in motion as the air and the pavement and the still
water are in motion
now I feel the world tugging on me from all directions I watch
dark flow tugging at the branches of a tree like a mama
tugging a jumper over her daughter's head
and the earth tugs at its root and the fiery wind beats its sides
now I see dark flow in the oat milk
now I see dark flow in the lime water

now I hear dark flow it has whooping cough
now I hear dark flow getting nostalgic about the nineties
I can hear it in the sound of my own footsteps
it is the cadence of our times
with each step it proposes a new aesthetic
each step brings me closer to visibility
each step is a completion of a natural choreography
make me visible
sodium lamps and nightclub LED and tanning bed UV and mobile
phone LCD are one big circulation of light
make me visible
now I am making a spring tonic from cleavers dandelion nettle
now I am waiting in my twelfth house for a new moon
now I chew my cuticles
now my back aches now I have indigestion now I can't
stop sneezing
now I see the flat needs dusting
when I first saw you I recognised you straight away
your eyes were my eyes
I said hello make me visible
I am waiting to serve you
let's propose a toast to extinction I said o but first make me visible
I am waiting to serve you
o now the night is over and here comes bert
o look at him with his rubbed eyes always with the allergies
o it's hard to love yourself with the things you know about yourself
the sun is on fire but somehow it stays
it is waiting to serve you
at the centre of its flame there is a coldness where nothing burns
or is that dark flow?
what even is dark flow?
is this it (does impression of dark flow)?
I'm going to imagine it as a horse
I'm going to picture it as the horse that keeps on going after
the jockey is thrown
look at it go

isn't it beautiful isn't it powerful isn't it fierce
did you ever see anything more alive?
I know how to get visible now
I know how to cast light
I know how to get visible now
I know how to cast light
but tell me paralyser forsaker rulebreaker
how to be unseen be uncast

A PREFIX

this is the price you pay

this is the price you pay

for living your life like a prefix

you were in love with

you were in love with the future

this is the price you pay

for living your life

like a prefix

what will be has been

what will be is being

what will be has become

this is your future a bad guitar solo

going on forever

a bad guitar solo going on forever

look around you

look around you do it now

the postman unbeknownst flaunts an earring of rain

no one knows what it all means

no one knows

this moment

take it

take this moment

take this moment that is being

take this moment that has been

take this moment and run it through a loop

take this moment and run it through a loop

look at how it improves with each repetition

look at how it is renewed

look at how with each repetition it is renewed

like Jerusalem it is renewed

like Jacob it is renewed

like the lizard's tail like blood like Britney

it is renewed

THE CONVULSION

we were a convulsion

we were a convulsion

that to some people

from a distance

looked like a dance

we were a convulsion that from a distance to some people
looked like a dance

but you know me, sweets
you know me, sweets

my throat

is crystal clear

and my spirit animal is the antelope

you know me, sweets

my throat is crystal clear and my spirit animal is the antelope

my heart is a convulsion

is a convulsion

I used to think there was a straight line

a straight line
you could trace

from the first kiss
to the long sleepless night

a straight line

as taut and inevitable as a lit firework

I used to think some things

I used to think some things like

if there was an afterlife
it would be dreamless

and therefore of no use to you or me

I used to think there was a straight line

from the dog to the stick

I used to think there was a straight line

from the match to the wick

I used to think there was a straight line

from the sun to the tan

from daydreaming to burnt soup

from the seed of doubt to the giant pumpkin of denial

and I used to think there was a hard-blowing gale

I used to think there was a hard-blowing gale

that drove me through the arcades

the lanes the arcades and the lanes and the arcades and
the lanes and the newspapers and the smell of pastry in a
hard-blowing gale

I used to think there was a hard-blowing gale

the newspapers and the smell of pastry and the lanes and
the arcades

to your bed

a hard-blowing gale

from me, to your bed

through whatever energy blew it

a story I told myself

but we were a convulsion

only a convulsion

a coffee jolt

a coffee jolt

you know me, sweets

I like coffee

and I am prey

like the antelope I am prey

you know me, sweets

my throat is crystal clear

you used to say you liked coffee how you liked your men

rich and Italian
rich and Italian

my heart and my throat

before our bodies went bloop
before our bodies went bloop

I used to think some things

that all turned out

all of them

all turned out to be false

and now I don't think those things

anymore

from a distance

we might have been dancing

from a distance

like we were dancing

from a distance

I used to think that too

I used to think that too

but sweets

there are no straight lines in nature

no blowing gale just for me

no straight lines in nature no blowing gale just for me
no straight lines in nature no blowing gale just for me

PAST EXTENDS

the past's a tightrope

are you with me?

the past's a tightrope

it extends

don't look down don't look back

the past grows

out of inertia

but look that was me, hey bert!

there I am locked out of the flat see how young and stupid I am!

she took the only key and went out dancing so
I couldn't go home

the past begins at home

the past extends out

I couldn't get in so I walked up into the hills of Llanhilleth

way up into the hills

my sad feet trudging up the hill

the past's a tightrope and this is me looking back

arms stretched out (that's rotational inertia)

I walked way up into those hills

and I sat with the trees

and there in the grass I saw a hock of spit with a feather in it

a hock of spit with a feather in it

the past's a tightrope and it's a mystery that's for sure

what holds it and where it goes and why

the tightrope's a mystery DON'T SHAKE IT!

keep going, biped
keep going

so I was up in the hills which were every shade of green I was
surrounded by trees and the more time I spent the more homely

but it was cold and getting dark so I gathered some twigs

I had my lighter so I lit a fire

and once I had it going I sat before it and looked into it
and I cried

I looked into the fire and cried

for all the selfish weakness of me I cried

for all the powerlessness that came from being unrooted I cried

and I cried because my heart was starving for love

and for the mystery of the tightrope I cried

for constructing a creation myth from her body I cried

and I sat there all night until dawn when the birds began to
stir and chatter and a slow drizzle fell and I jerked off
stamped out what embers were left of the fire and I walked
the trail until it descended into the valley

all was emptiness

a hock of spit with a feather in it

the past's a tightrope

so find your centre of gravity

your own centre of gravity, got it, biped?

everything behind you is inert

everything behind you is no longer yours

LIONHEART

Now, whenever anyone mentions your name
I say it back, stunned,
as if it were some old song I never
expected anyone else
to know.

I imagine you as a cartoon coyote
falling off a cliff
or holding onto
a stick of dynamite. I see you

gazing out at the parrots on Telegraph Hill
a sudden tourist
somewhere in your thirties.

Watering your plants,
mourning roadkill.

Hypnotised by your own samsara.

You were younger than Eve, you were
weaker than Adam. You were doomed as the
fallen armies were doomed,
and the armies returning home
to their beds,
their crucifixes,

their strange lovers.

SHOW HOMES

My mum and dad loved show homes.
Every Sunday we'd get in the car and go.

We saw so many show homes growing up
that my brother and I invented a game called *Estate Agents*.

He'd show me around our own house saying things like
This is the living room
Very spacious, I'd say
Yes, and this is the window
Lovely view

We'd stand there looking out at the neighbour's bins.

AND NO GENERATION WON

when you fell

I heard the break of waves

the ocean like a roll of film
unspooled

you are the sound

of waves

suspended

the sound

of the ocean

self-preserving

we sat together watching seagulls in history
we sat together watching seagulls in history

your ear on tarmac

listening

for what the tarmac discloses

it didn't concern me

something that didn't concern me

you were the puppet

that broke its own strings

for the sake of

the act of

falling

you fell

I saw you fall
and no generation won

when it came to decay

no generation won

now something between us has been dismantled

a memory I have yet to retrieve

tonight

a memory

the sound of waves breaking

lies somewhere ahead of you

somewhere ahead of you

the lies you will tell

the lies you will have to tell to someone new

for the sake of

intimacy

the insinuation of beauty

the act of falling

while the place we inhabit

refuses

to reveal itself

the place we inhabit refuses

maybe
falling is a form of self-preservation

when it comes to decay

maybe this is how we get through

this is how we get through

maybe this is how we get through

we expel the

world

from ourselves

THE PRIMARY BRIDE

On the walk home;
because there is nothing but information we are all informers
(you and Anna had been drinking since midday)

Halfway over the Eden Bridge you stopped, you are a sucker
for the German Romantics.
Neon twinkling river,

      in the distance the floodlit.
      (your hair too, sepia angularis)

Anna and I knew each other years ago, art college, Leeds.
You had been, now were again, might
well be tomorrow,
in love
with Anna.

We looked out over the bridge, startled, I put an arm
around your shoulder.
The post-rock era wept behind us.

Yes sir, look! I said,
see how the river consummates the despair!

YOUTH

it must be wild in some way

if not sacred
at least less tangled

sitting here on a zafu
looking out at the rain

I was once the star-humper
I was so goddamn beautiful
you could not have ignored me then

BELLY

THE CONTENTS OF A HUMAN BODY

my father taught me silence

I'll never see my father again, probably
I'll never see my father again

papa's death is a mountain I keep looking up at
papa's death is a bear I keep feeding
papa bought me a wristwatch with one of those acid house smiley
faces on it but mama pulled it offa me
mama pulled the acid house smiley face wristwatch offa me

she threw it across the room
and he went like this

smack

he went like this

smack

he went like this

smack

on mama's face

and I couldn't tell the time yet
I couldn't tell the time

and I'll never see my father again, probably
but I feel him inside me and I see him in the mirror
and in the mirror I say to myself *better brush those teeth bert*

better brush those teeth bert if you don't want them to rot

better floss those teeth bert
if you don't want them to rot

when I first left home (I hadn't seen my father for some years
even then)
when I first left home my dad would visit me in dreams

in these dreams he would lay his warm hand on my forehead
and
he never said a word

just like in life he never said a word

and I would wake up and I would be in this new city

I would wake up and look around at my new room
and it was so lonely

my father taught me silence

my father taught me the silence of men

shhhh listen

listen to it

I have become one of those men

those men who indulge through silence their own shhhh *victimhood*

their own shhhh *immortal victimhood*

my own shhhh *immortal silence*

my father taught me the human body

the human body is made up of:

70% silence
20% coffee
10% slow dancing

I read somewhere that when we dream everyone in our dreams is us

everyone in your dreams is you

you are some part of everyone in your dreams

papa's death is the monument that keeps sinking
papa's death is the recipe I can't get right

according to the internet the smiley face icon can be traced back to 1963 where it was used on a kid's TV show in America, the show was called The Funny Company *and that was their logo. The show's catchphrase was 'Keep Smiling'.*

lay your warm hand on my forehead Franco
lay your warm hand on my lonely forehead

my father the hairdresser you should see him with scissors
you should see him with scissors his pinky finger out like that
you should see him

I probably won't ever see him again

keep smiling papa keep smiling through the silence
and *Rai Uno* and tooth-rot
keep smiling

and feel the silence inside you like smoke

annoying isn't it

does it feel like choking
does it feel like shrinking

shhhh
listen

keep listening
can you hear it? can you hear it papa?

you are in this room

I have felt you the holy man moving through the hallway with
muddy boots you are the backbone walker your third eye
is always dry you take deep inhalations of the blood-scented air
look up at the murmurations of starlings touch feathery down

you are the ivy up on top of me no one could subtract you from
your stem you are old summers on fields of Hypnum and grey
stone you are the cold wind in my attic you wake
me up with your TV light

I knew you when you were a mountain when you were
my mountain celestial vomit of the untuned atom
oh years of my blood blood of my years

insect walker
insect walker

you were in this room just now
you were in this room so far so far
the room is so far so far

the floorboards creak beneath your ordinary boots

your warm hand on my forehead
your warm hand on my forehead

ONE FISH

let's pretend everything is as it should be

everything is as it should be

everything is as it should be

as it should be

say it with me

there is only one fish
in selfish

there is only one fish
in selfish

every fish is as it should be

every fish is as it should be

say it with me

don't get personal with me
don't get physical with me

these headaches
these headaches I've been having

these headaches are the selfish trying to get out

these headaches are the selfish
trying to bust out

let's pretend I am as I should be

I am as I should be
I am as I should be

I am I am I am
I am I am I am

say it with me

you are you are you are
we are we are we are

you knead me

I knead you

this world
this world

get personal with me
get physical with me

this world

knead me like I knead you

my head

say it with me

these headaches are the fish trying to swim out

trying to swim out

I knead you

say it with me

I knead you

to swim

PINK LIGHT

open a window

now reach your arms out through the window

stretch your arms all the way around the house across the
road from yours

pull the house towards you

now climb out through your window into the window of the
other house

gather the inhabitants of the house around you

they are your family now

ask them to hold you tight

ask them to hold you tight

while in their embrace
dehusk

dehusk

now your new family are embracing only your husk

now you are pink light

a shining pink light

go out into the town

find a car

go out into the town

pink light find car

a fast car to synthesise with

when you have found the car start it with your pink light

now you are an automaton

you are an automaton going fast

you are an automaton hurtling through the dark

you are natural now

you have returned to nature

all the motorway is charged with your pink light

the motorway is suffused with a pink glowing haze and you
are everywhere

and you are beautiful

now close the window

feel that emotion

KNOCKING FROM THE HERE ALONE

Oh Potential! I hear you knocking

could you knock
a little louder

a little louder

remove the softness from your softness

if I told you something true
about desire

something true about desire

something true

if I pulled it out and showed you

how the rain makes me dry up

with desire

how your death affirmations soften me

with desire

keep moving the softness into softness

Oh Unrealised!
Oh Wasted!

I leave the door ajar

the door ajar

for you

I leave the door ajar

I pull this true thing out unrecognisable to you

I pull this true thing out

to confirm my lack of loneliness
I rehearse my lack of loneliness

I wait

as the day after tomorrow waits

we wait for each other

hey, monday

hey, bert

hey, tuesday

hey, bert

hey, wednesday

hey, bert

hey, thursday

hey, bert

hey, friday

hey, bert wanna party?

no thanks, friday

hey, saturday

hey, bert

hey, sunday

hey, bert

don't unsoften the softness

from the here alone

I rehearse your crowded rejection

I confirm your crowded rejection

I plant my hands in the earth and I water them

I plant my hands in the earth and I water them

I am softly beholden

I hold on softly

NEW BOY

What you doing new boy?

just looking for my friend

What you doing new boy?

looking for my only friend

You following me new boy?

I'm just looking for my buddy

I think you were looking for me new boy

I think you were looking for me

friendship is a harbour

I am twelve years old and friendship is a harbour

now time is like chewing-gum

but back then friendship was a harbour

I think I saw him in here

she says

I think I saw him in here

Ohh anyone?

she calls out

Ohh anyone??

it happens this way

in the computer room at break-time

it happened like this

she undid my tie and her hand reached down

Ohhh anyone??

I am twelve years old and no one has touched it yet

she pulls my zip down

and I am like the hulk

a startling metamorphosis occurs

I am like the hulk a startling metamorphosis occurs

I run hastily outta there

Ohhh anyone??

I run out of the computer room right outta there

Ohhh anyone??

I run down the stairs two by two

Ohhh anyone??

I am new boy

Ohhh anyone??

I am new boy and no one has touched it yet

now time is like chewing-gum

but back then friendship was a harbour

now when anyone touches it
I go *Ohhh anyone??*

I go *Ohhh anyone??*

I get them to say it with me

I get them to say it

we go *Ohhh anyone??*

when they touch it I make them say *Ohhh anyone??*

Ohhh anyone?? like that

like when friendship was a harbour

I make them say *Ohhh anyone??*
like when friendship was a harbour

and I hear Melissa laughing

I hear Melissa laughing at me

now friendship looks elsewhere

now friendship looks elsewhere

and time is like chewing-gum

and now when someone touches it I go *Ohhh anyone??*

now when someone touches me there I go *Ohhh anyone??*

I go *Ohhh anyone??*

like when I was new boy

Melissa is a hairdresser now

she works in a hair salon

I said Melissa is a hairdresser she works in a hair salon

and I go in there and I get my head shaved

and she gets the clippers and she wraps a towel around me

she wraps a towel around me and she gets the clippers and
she shaves my head

and she puts her hands on my scalp
this is what she does

she puts her hands on my scalp and presses gently
and this is how I know what her hands feel like

this is how I know what her hands feel like finally

she presses them so gently on my scalp

and I let her

I let her

and my little shaved hairs get on the backs of her hands

and they mingle with the hairs on her arms

they want to be there

the backs of her hands
the hairs on her arms

when she's done she brushes them off

she brushes them off

she brushes my hair off

and time is like chewing-gum

and friendship looks elsewhere

and when I get home I can still hear her saying

Ohhh anyone??

I touch my scalp and she is saying

Ohhh anyone??

and I am new boy

Ohhh anyone??

and she is laughing and she is laughing and she is laughing

PARADISE ISLAND

it was just the two of us on this Paradise Island

the sky was so blue and the sea was so green
and every day she would lay a blanket on the sand
and she'd say *I'm going to catch some D*

I'm going to catch some D
here on this Paradise Island

and when the sun set she'd say
My skin feels like melted butter

My skin feels like melted butter here on this Paradise Island
it was just the two of us and the blue so blue sky and the
green so green sea

and no one could get to us and no one knew we were there

there were no phones on our Paradise Island
and no post office
and no one could get to us and no one knew we were there

in the evening we drank martinis and watched the sun set

and she'd say *Tomorrow I'm going to catch some D*

no one could find us
and anyway who would be looking?

we had left behind no trace
our lives had left no trace and it was Paradise

This is Paradise she said
I even understand what the toucans are saying

I understand the language of the toucans she said
Here on this Paradise Island

The toucans say we are mistaken about the most basic
principles of life
The toucans say we have everything upside down and
inside out

Sky on Bird, they say. Sea on Fish
SKY ON BIRD. SEA ON FISH

now I am at home remembering the Paradise Island and telling everyone I know
about the Paradise Island and everyone is sick of hearing about it and I keep
telling them they have everything upside down and inside out and even their basic
principles of life are wrong and that they are unarmed by conception, you are
unarmed by conception I tell them, you are indebted to silence, to the great silence,
you cannot hear the toucans and your eyes aren't right colours and you cannot see
right colours and everything is silent and dichromatic, everything is silent and
dichromatic SKY ON BIRD SEA ON FISH SKY ON BIRD SEA ON FISH

it was just the two of us on this Paradise Island

you said *The toucans are glad we are here*
catching some D

and I'd look into your eyes on our Paradise Island
and your eyes would be so so brown

So brown I'd say *So, so BROWN!!*

and at the end of each day
you'd say *My skin feels like melted butter*

Like butter, like MELTED BUTTER!!
and the toucans would say
(the croaking of toucans)

(more croaking)

SKY ON BIRD
SEA ON FISH

VIVIAN SLEEPING

the lady led you into her room

with a rose in her hand
a cross dangling

at her throat

and Vivian sleeping

and she showed you Vivian sleeping
and the yellows and blues in her blanket

the flicker of her lids

and her creases
and her fragrance

she showed you Vivian sleeping

like a leopard in space

fingers clutching
her pillow

and her black and white alsatian
asleep too in the corner

dribbling

the lady
reached across

removed Vivian's blanket

and left

leaving you
paralysed

alone in a room
with naked Vivian sleeping

exposed
exposed

sleeping

and when she wakes how will you explain it to her this time?

what will you say?
will you quote Caliban again?

My mistress show'd me thee, and thy dog and thy bush.

JUDAS STEER

his avalanche won't harm you

when it comes

it might sound like a covenant

i have held onto these secrets for you

i will hold onto these secrets for you

it might sound like a covenant

it is an abandonment

he is the abandoner

and he will have a heart like a judas steer

he will tremble with anticipation when the telephone rattles

he will never be still
he will never be still

and you will be barely aware of your defeat

like the hypnotic echo of a man constantly recoiling

he will be indiscernible from the distance through which
he has drawn you

his love was a snail smudge across the air

in the end you will blame fate
or something anything yourself

and you will understand this man by the things he leaves behind

his conversation will cling to your surroundings

lingering, taking up space

the space you meant to do something important with

it will always be cluttered

you will walk through it looking for misplaced things

you will lose your way

when you go into town for groceries you will have the look of
someone trapped inside a cupboard

because of this man you will always be known for
what you are missing

you will be the unscrewed jar

the anchoress

the betrayed calf

in the blizzard of your bed sheets you will always be fishing

HOW TO TAKE A BATH

run the water

remove your clothes

step into the water

remove your pink light

submerge your whole body in the water

remove your suffering

THE TRICK WITH FLIES

The hotel mirror is so clean you cannot fathom why you feel
so dirty.

The fly at the lightbulb is trying to get home but cannot fathom
why home would burn like that.

You hold your belly, tell it
you were conceived in tenderness,
on a planet that was coming apart at the seams.

You thought maybe the child growing inside you
was an incarnation of your own mother. That all you'd ever
be able to create was a reproduction of that which had created you.

The trick with flies, your mother used to say
is to never let them feel at home.

A NEXT TIME

Easy passage in.
Easy passage out.

A decent interval between, enough
to not have to think about it.
All debts restaurant bills and inherited guilt paid in full.
All the stones that filled up your pockets along the way, tossed
back.
The way the blanket covers your body and
warms you, activating that good vagus nerve.

Morning coffee at Lufkin, looking out at a morning
so full of expectation that it reminds you of being a virgin and
staying up late listening to the radio with your brother.

There is sunshine on the windows but the clouds are coming in.
There is a cat under a car,
birds caw-cawing on the chimney tops.

Picking up beans and potatoes on your way home and the rain
holds out and when you get in you remember there is no
work tomorrow and there is a fresh jug of lime water in the fridge.

I wish all these things for you.

I wish you
deep sleep
clean air
good books.

Touching and being
touched.

Whatever drug takes you there.

A next time for each thing.

HEART

JUST SO YOU KNOW

I'm on my way over
in my favourite blue pyjamas
to rip that novel from your head.

CHRISTMASTIME IN BUTE PARK

Frost covers the grass.
You and I sit and watch the dogs,
the men and women in yellow coats
stringing up the lights.
You are confused by the out-of-scale reindeer.

We are warming our cupped hands on the take-away
coffee still too burny to drink,
black and steaming, you look peaceful, watching
those lights go up.

Frost covers the grass,
the coffee scalds, the dogs play, then, and this never
gets old, the night is lit up.
I sit here,
thankful that all my friends who have tried to kill themselves
so far have failed.

YOU WERE THE ONLY ONE I WOULD'VE STAYED BEHIND FOR WHEN I KNEW IT WAS TIME TO GO

Caro amico, it's been a while. So. How are you now?
I was just sitting here at this table
watching the streetlight flashing on and off then on
then off again like some holy Morse Code spelling out
your name, and it occurs to me
I don't know the last time I even spoke your name out loud. *Huh.*
Are you still living in Denmark? Are you still pissed at me? I was
a shitty friend, sorry.

You were the only witness to
the hormonal Jane-fixated Ventolin years. My first cigarette.
First kiss. You were what, maybe nineteen,
when you told me you'd eloped but
you didn't want your parents to find out. Listening to
Donovan in your brown Nova looking for a place to smoke.
I loved you then, with no sense of time running out. But you
were married and I hadn't even met the girl, and what
was I supposed to say.

Then she flew back to America and never came home.
And you punched your fist through the windshield.

Secretly, I was glad. Anyway is that even how it really happened?
It's been years and I've begun to doubt my own memories.
How are you? You tried to die. I spoke to your dad
about it on the phone, this was while you were in the hospital,
he told me an older woman had been involved, and for
some reason this whole time I've pictured her
as Joan Crawford.
(I just pulled a spirit animal oracle for you, it came up hawk)
I suppose I should've written your number

down somewhere before you left the country, I could've
said all this in person but yada yada it's been years, maybe
we've changed. Anything we'd have to say to each other now
is probably best kept to ourselves, right? We used to
tell each other everything.

Anyway, I got out. And here in Cardiff my life has
gotten small, but somehow, you'll never believe this, I fell
in love with a woman who (wait for it) loves me back.
In a lot of ways though, I don't feel all that different.
I still sit around at home all day doing nothing, still stare at my
feet when I walk through town, still prefer the company of animals.
I miss you and keep you with me. *What thou lovest*
well remains; something that Ezra Pound wrote. We were
born five days apart. We were twenty-one, waiting for a bus
because the summer was over. I left that town with a
broken heart and a gash over my right eye
which you gave me, but it was an accident you said.

Tell me buddy, *que pasa?*
Purveyor of laced after-dinner snacks,
slurrer of bad nineties lyrics under moonlight, brother of chalk, sister
of ash, stalker of rare birds in the bluebell woods,
oh shoulder of my sighs, oh river bed
oh forge of Pisces
oh keeper of all my secrets
oh first lost.

THERE IS A WORLD BELOW

When you're clinging to the edge of the world
don't be afraid to fall,
there is a world below.

There is a world below, a living thing
where debris like us
can settle.

You have made no allegiances
to this false construction,
there are no buff lawmen patrolling
your inner jurisdiction.
It is a monolith you have been clinging to
that you knew was coming down,
let go,
there is a world below.

There are many graves you have already tended to,
their message sits
like a beard upon your heart.
Your stomach resembles a tangle of Christmas lights
that each year gets
harder to unravel.

There is a world below, a living thing
where you can brush the leaves
from out of the books you've been
nesting in.
Where you can reach into the TV screen
and pull out
another disillusioned hand,
same as yours.

When you're clinging to the edge of the world
don't be afraid to fall,
there is a world below.

THEN AGAIN

you are a place   where I hold on

I don't know if time became the opposition because we
gave it a name
I don't know if death is a performance we are actively
involved in

the end credits go on for so long

there is a state of being   and a state of non-being   also a state
of statelessness

then again, there is a matchstick in my heart   and a zithering
in my manipura

when I close my eyes I imagine myself on an empty beach
it is 1978   I am sitting cross-legged on a blanket on the sand
the sand is a beautiful mustard yellow

the tide is coming in   I am breathing into my abdomen
if we decide something is real...
then again, some things must be only ideas

like the crystal cave guided meditation we did last night   I was
worried that if I became too open to suggestion   I might spend
the rest of my life in there

or what if the cave was real and all these years were a
guided visualisation   I hear his voice   telling me about
the light   asking me to let it   enter my head

it doesn't sound entirely unlike me

then again, you are the only place   I want to hold on to

THIS DECISIVE ARC

I will not forget you

I will not forget you

imagine that

when I inhabit the rose
and the season discharges within me

when I inhabit the rose

I will know what this intermission means

has meant

my bed is warm

I move from this decisive arc
where our love first flared

to the morning
of our torn light

I will not forget you

if I ever did

the mother and child might fold
into each other

the mother and child might fold

you could place your hand on the wound
and your hand would be fucked

you could place your hand on the wound

and your hand

and you could cup your hand

you could cup your hand around the sound we made

the sound we made

the sound we made was so loud
the sound we made was so loud

it comes back

sometimes

the sound we made

comes back

faint but it comes

like distant chatter

beneath the residue of my own voice

of my own voice when I am speaking

beneath the residue of my own voice when I am speaking

carelessly

carelessly when I am speaking

HEART POEM

Recently I get this sense, maybe you feel it too, of
time circling back on itself; or if not time, which is only
really air isn't it, sometimes you move through it with ease,
unblemished, like new, like this, and sometimes, well
you know; if *not* time, then
some unrighteous angst that seemed to infect our generation,
like an abscess that kept getting bigger, itchier
through the years, and which
for so long nagged me, somehow contracting,
peeling off like an onion skin, revealing
this rapturous sluglike substance which might be my actual heart.
It is as though a window has been opened and
some old familiar scent once lost to me, like the smell of
an old school bag, has drifted in;
into this room I'm in and this body I'm in, renewed
by some grand emotional migration. And if, my butterbean,
every day of our life together isn't all golden, and if
not every meal, sleep, or poem, is as good as
it could be, that's okay. We're good.
Elizabeth Hardwick wrote *This is what I have decided to do*
with my life just now, and this is what I have decided
to do with mine. And you with yours.
Not everything can be *Witchita Lineman*. Not everything must
aspire to greatness. Sometimes just enough is
solid. The basil and sage need watering, I'll fill up
the can. This morning in the courtyard
the neighbour's old raggedy dog looked me right
in the eyes and really straight through them into the private
self-grieving ego of my all-too-humanness. It is a fine day.
Because life is short, we all
die young.

INFUSE WITH CHAMOMILE, LAVENDER & CATNIP

These last months I've been trying to
grow lemon balm from seed. Little pots on all
the window sills. It is a small experiment in living, kindness, while
I have no sense of purpose.
I read about cultivars and powdery mildew. Somewhere
in the middle of it all I find myself cuffed
to the wrists of your hair. Fumbling around the basement
I stumble upon a box filled with your hair. At night I dream of
stabbing a fork into a bowl of it, twirling it around like spaghetti
and scoffing it down.
It's true, I just wanted this world. To feel a bit more. Like home.
My old art teacher used to say, when you're feeling
listless make a list. I make a list of the things that help me
feel rooted. Cats, Beetroot, *Dynasty*, *Wild*, Bob Dylan,
Time With Siân.
These periods of flatness are okay, I entrust them,
I too am an experiment in living, and kindness. I know
what's in the basement, I love everything above and below.
Never again will I refute joy. Never again will my heart be a
mechanical claw in a lonely arcade. What I lack
in ambition, I try to make up for in devotion.
I take my pots of sprouting lemon balm out for a walk,
we enjoy all the rank smells of summer. I describe
the sky to them: *blue and transparent,* I say
blue and transparent.

YOU GET USED TO IT

Waiting for the tea to mash. No major
revelations here, though I will say this;
that sometimes these days I look back and half-heartedly find
my young life fairly endearing, and at forty I know
I'm a late-bloomer.
Pressing the teabag into the edge of the mug, letting that
last bit of darkness seep in, plunking the used bag into the bowl,
just a splash of milk, I like oat milk best. Then taking it
into the living room, placing it on the *Rockford Files* coaster
on the arm of the sofa, and sitting down. I fought for all this.
I did fight. Not in any real sense, you understand. But still. It was
real to me. And much stronger people than I (almost everyone is
by the way, not in all the ways but in a lot of ways), have been
crushed under the years, or they've gone weird, or their lights
have, y'know, I guess dimmed, the ol' faderoo.
They'd probably try to convince me that my happiness
is wilful ignorance. Listen, I know the world is a shitstorm.
I know the animals suffer and cannot speak. I know how
every embodiment of the human form is diminished. I know
about the slow vandalisms of the heart. I know my happiness
is a kind of compromise, I could do more.
I open the window a little. Sit back down. Take a sip of the tea,
still hot. It was about twenty years ago I climbed that tree
to try and impress Laura, why I thought it would god knows.
It was after the club shut, it was the end of October.
There I was in this tree. I wasn't sure how to get down.
The wind was drying my dancing-sweat, there were
no leaves on the branches and the moon was big and yellow,
and there she was
passed out on the grass below.

AN ENDLESS SUPPLY

Before this spring
we hung crystals at our bedroom window. Now when
we wake, rainbows tremble all around us
and they are really quite lovely
and each morning it's as though they've multiplied.

Each day is warmer than the last. I sleep
with my tush out, one leg over the blanket.
I dream of attics and lifts and
hotels with long corridors and plush staircases
and you could say my love for you
grows exponentially. You could say that the sun
doesn't set, we reject its light. Knowing

there will always be more.
That there is in fact an almost endless supply
of light. I think that's also how things are with us.
But just to be safe
let's keep nourishing this thing, let's not
let the days go by too easily.

Tonight, penguin, when we switch off our
bedside lamps, I plan to hold my eyes open for a little while longer,
just a few seconds longer, and then it's business as usual,
I'll close them,
slip an arm around you, slide the other
under my pillow, that's all. Goodnight.

FINALLY

the function of the kiss is silence

THIS ONE THING

I must've ridden a pony once
anyway
I half-remember doing so
I was maybe three years old and I must've ridden
that animal around for a while

the years and the buttocks
flatten out
the years and the heart
get sloppy

black obsidian
lime water
dusty sheets

let the world go on spitting teeth
let the old men rant until they choke
let them castrate the forests the oceans the bright magnificent sky
let us all be defeated in the end

they crucified love and keep crucifying love
those old men, were they
never young?
did they never perform that loneliest of invocations to
someone *anyone* in the middle of the night?
did they never fall to pieces at the supermarket in the
frozen food aisle for no reason and because of nothing?
did they never ride a pony with a heart so small and
so flung wide open?

let them win
but remember this one thing
inside you a country is burning

it is the country from which they are exiled

NOTES

EPIGRAPH
This collection's epigraph by Michelle Stuart is from *Overlay: Contemporary Art and the Art of Prehistory* by Lucy R. Lippard (The New Press, New York, 1983)

VIVIAN SLEEPING
The Caliban quote referenced is from William Shakespeare, *The Tempest* Pg. 56, Act II Sc. II (The RSC Shakespeare, Macmillan Publishers, 2008).

YOU WERE THE ONLY ONE I WOULD'VE STAYED BEHIND FOR WHEN I KNEW IT WAS TIME TO GO
The poem quotes from 'Canto LXXXI', *The Cantos of Ezra Pound* (New Directions, 1999).

HEART POEM
The Elizabeth Hardwick line is from 'Writing a Novel', *The New York Review* (Oct 1973, Vol 20, No. 16).

THANKS

To everyone at Parthian, especially my friend and editor Susie Wildsmith, for believing in me and making this book better. To Molly Sinclair-Thomson, who also listens to the toucans. To Amanda Ataou, Gosia Buzzanca, Susan Evans, Crystal Jeans, Owain Lewis, Amy Mason, Laura McNutt, and Clover Peake, for all the good advice, support, and friendship. To my mama, always. To Nick Pemberton, again, who once told me, totally misquoting Smokey Robinson, that a taste of love is better than none at all. And to my wife, Siân, thank you thank you thank you.

PARTHIAN *Poetry in Translation*

Home on the Move
Two poems go on a journey
Edited by Manuela Perteghella
and Ricarda Vidal
ISBN 978-1-912681-46-4
£8.99 | Paperback
'One of the most inventive and necessary
poetry projects of recent years...'
– Chris McCabe

Pomegranate Garden
A selection of poems by Haydar Ergülen
Edited by Mel Kenne, Saliha Paker
and Caroline Stockford
ISBN 978-1-912681-42-6
£8.99 | Paperback
'A major poet who rises from [his] roots to touch
on what is human at its most stripped-down,
vulnerable and universal...'
– Michel Cassir, *L'Harmattan*

Modern Bengali Poetry
Arunava Sinha
ISBN 978-1-912681-22-8
£11.99 | Paperback
This volume celebrates over one hundred years
of poetry from the two Bengals represented
by over fifty different poets.

PARTHIAN *Poetry*

Hey Bert
Roberto Pastore
ISBN 978-1-912109-34-0
£9.00 | Paperback
'Bert's writing, quite simply, makes me happy.
Jealous but happy.'
– Crystal Jeans

Sliced Tongue and Pearl Cufflinks
Kittie Belltree
ISBN 978-1-912681-14-3
£9.00 | Paperback
'By turns witty and sophisticated, her writing shivers
with a suggestion of unease that is compelling.'
– Samantha Wynne-Rhydderch

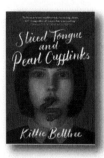

Hymns Ancient & Modern
New & Selected Poems
J. Brookes
ISBN 978-1-912681-33-4
£9.99 | Paperback
'It's a skilful writer indeed who can combine elements both
heartbreaking and hilarious: Brookes is that writer.'
– Robert Minhinnick

The Filthy Quiet
Kate Noakes
ISBN 978-1-91-268102-0
£8.99 | Paperback
'Kate Noakes' *The Filthy Quiet* is ... always
brightly striking onwards, generating
its own irresistible energy.'
– Jane Commane